DARTH VADER™

and Family
COLORING BOOK

CHRONICLE BOOKS
SAN FRANCISCO

D1401862

ISBN 978-1-4521-5923-2

Manufactured in China

MIX
Paper from
responsible sources
FSC™ C104723
FSC
www.fsc.org

Written and drawn by Jeffrey Brown
Designed by Michael Morris
Production Assistance by Kristoffer Branco

Thanks to Steve Mockus, J. W. Rinzler, Marc Gerald, Michael
Morris, and my family. Special thanks to Ryan Germick and
Micheal Lopez at Google for the original inspiration to make
Darth Vader and Son. Most of all, thanks to George Lucas for
making great toys and letting me play with them.

10 9 8 7 6 5 4 3 2 1

Chronicle Books LLC
680 Second Street
San Francisco, CA 94107
www.chroniclebooks.com

www.starwars.com

Chronicle books and gifts are available at special quantity discounts to corporations,
professional associations, literacy programs, and other organizations. For details
and discount information, please contact our premiums department at
corporatesales@chroniclebooks.com or at 1-800-759-0190.

PETTING ZOO